CONTENTS

Witches' Freaky Fingers

These freaky cheese straw fingers with pecan nails even have bloodstained ends to really give you the shivers! Don't be too scared—it's only ketchup.

MAKES 20

+ 1 cap (115g) cheddar cheese
+ 1 cap, plus 2 tablespoons (140g) all-purpose flour
+ 3 tablespoons (40g) butter
+ Pinch of salt
+ ½ teaspoon cayenne pepper
+ 1 egg, beaten
+ 2 tablespoons olive oil
+ 1 tablespoon chopped fresh parsley
+ Tomato ketchup, for dipping
+ About 1⅓ cap (35g) pecans

1 Grate the cheese. Put the flour, butter (cut into 3–4 pieces), salt, and pepper in a food processor and blend, using a pulsation action, until the mixture forms bread crumbs. Add the cheese and half of the egg and blend until combined.

2 Turn the dough onto a lightly floured counter and knead lightly together. Divide into 20 pieces and roll each piece into a 4-inch (10cm) finger. Put the fingers on a large cookie sheet and, with your fingers, press the centers of each to look like knuckles. Brush with beaten egg, reserving a little for later. Put in the refrigerator for 30 minutes until firm.

3 Preheat the oven to 350°F/180°C/fan 160°C/ Gas Mark 4. Bake the fingers in the oven for 10 minutes.

4 Meanwhile, mix together the oil and parsley. Remove the fingers from the oven, brush with the parsley mixture, and dip one end of each finger into tomato ketchup to look like blood. Using beaten egg to secure them in place, press a pecan in the other end of each finger to look like nails.

5 Return to the oven and bake for an additional 10 minutes until golden brown. Let cool before serving.

MARSHMALLOW SKELETONS

YOU WILL NEED

+ 8 large and 44 small white marshmallows
+ Toothpicks
+ Chocolate writing icing

MAKES 2

Thread three large marshmallows onto a wooden skewer to make the body. Add two mini marshmallows to make the neck and one large marshmallow for the head. Thread about five mini marshmallows onto two toothpicks to make the arms. Repeat to make the legs and feet. Stick the toothpicks into the body of the skeleton. Using the writing icing, pipe dots onto the skeleton to look like eyes. If you have more marshmallows, repeat until you run out of time or marshmallows!

Quick MAKE

SLIMY SLITHERING JELLIES

Quick MAKE

YOU WILL NEED

+ *Two 5-ounce (140g) packages lime gelatin dessert*
+ *A selection of jelly candies, such as crocodiles, fish, frogs, scorpions, snails, snakes, turtles, worms*

SERVES 6

Make up the gelatin following the package directions. Pour half of the liquid into six 7-ounce (200ml) clear plastic pots or glasses. Add three or four jelly candies to each container and then put in the refrigerator and leave for about 1 hour until set. Keep the remaining gelatin at room temperature. When the gelatin has set, add the rest of the gelatin to the pots or glasses and add another three or four jelly candies. Put them at the side of the containers so that they stick out of the gelatin and hang them over the edges so that they look as though they are escaping. Return to the refrigerator and leave for about 1 hour, until set. Serve with extra candies on top.

Bloodshot Eyes

MAKES 8

+ 4 extra large eggs
+ 2 tablespoons mayonnaise
+ Green food coloring
+ 4 black olives
+ Red food coloring

Eyes that stare at you can be scary, especially when they're bloodshot, but these are harmless and good to eat! Fill boiled eggs with creepy green-colored yolks topped with black olives, and streak with food coloring to create your own eerie eyeballs.

1 Put the eggs in a saucepan, cover with cold water, and slowly bring to a boil. Immediately reduce the heat and simmer gently for 10 minutes. As soon as the eggs are cooked, drain and put under cold running water until cool. Gently crack the shells and leave until completely cold. When cold, crack the shells all over and remove them.

2 Slice a small piece of egg white off each side of the eggs and set aside. Slice each egg in half. Scoop out the egg yolks, put in a bowl, and add the mayonnaise. Mash together until smooth.

3 Dip the tip of a skewer into the green food coloring, add to the egg yolks, and stir until evenly colored. Spoon the mixture back into the center of the egg whites.

4 Place the reserved egg white slices in the middle. Cut the olives in half and place, cut side down, on top of the sliced egg whites to make the center of the eye.

5 Dip the tip of a skewer into the red food coloring and draw streaks onto the eyes to look like bloodshot eyes.

Wizards' Trick-or-Treat Cupcakes

The Halloween rhyme, "Trick or treat, smell my feet, give me something good to eat" is only three-quarters true for this recipe! Red velvet cupcakes are filled with either chocolate or blue cheese! Have a treat ready for those that are unlucky enough to bite into a trick cupcake.

MAKES 12

- ½ cup (125ml) buttermilk
- 1 tablespoon red liquid food coloring
- ½ cup/1 stick (115g) butter, softened
- 1 cup (175g) superfine sugar
- ½ teaspoon vanilla extract
- 1 extra large egg
- 1⅔ cups (200g) all-purpose flour
- 1 tablespoon unsweetened cocoa
- ½ teaspoon baking soda
- 1½ teaspoons white wine vinegar

FOR THE FILLING

- 1½ ounces (40g) blue cheese
- 6 tablespoons chocolate spread

FOR THE TOPPING

- 9 tablespoons (125g) butter, softened
- 2 cups (250g) confectioners' sugar
- 1 tablespoon milk
- Orange food coloring
- Mini sugar-coated chocolates, sugar sprinkles, or Halloween cake toppers, to decorate

1 Preheat the oven to 350°F/180°C/
fan 160°C/Gas Mark 4. Line a muffin
pan with 12 paper muffin cases.

2 Mix together the buttermilk and
food coloring.

3 Using an electric mixer, whisk
together the butter, superfine sugar,
and vanilla extract in a large bowl
until light and fluffy. Gradually beat in
the egg. Sift in the flour and cocoa, fold
into the mixture, and then stir in the
buttermilk. Mix the baking soda and
vinegar together and then stir into the
batter. Spoon the batter evenly into
the muffin cases.

4 Bake the cakes in the oven for 25
minutes until firm to the touch.
Transfer to a wire rack and let cool.

5 When the cakes are cold, use a teaspoon to
scoop out a 1-inch (2.5cm) hole from the
center of each cupcake and set aside. Use
the teaspoon to remove a little more cake
from each hole to allow room for the filling.

6 Divide the blue cheese into three pieces
and use to fill the holes of three cakes. Use
the chocolate spread to fill the holes of the
remaining cakes. Replace the reserved cake
in the holes of the cakes to plug them.

7 To make the topping, put the butter in
a large bowl and, using an electric mixer,
whisk until light and fluffy. Sift in the
confectioners' sugar, add the milk, and mix
together by hand until combined. Dip the
tip of a skewer into the food coloring, add
to the mixture, and whisk until smooth
and evenly colored.

8 Using a round-bladed knife, swirl the
topping on top of the cakes to cover.
Add the decoration of your choice.

BANANA GHOSTS

Quick **MAKE**

YOU WILL NEED

+ 4 small bananas
+ Chocolate writing icing

MAKES 8

Cut the bananas in half widthwise. Using chocolate writing icing, make eyes and a mouth. Serve at once or brush with lemon juice to stop the bananas turning brown. Alternatively, dip in melted white chocolate. Let set and add chocolate chips for eyes and a mouth.

A BAG OF BONES

YOU WILL NEED

+ 4 breadsticks
+ 12 large white marshmallows
+ 6 ounces (175g) compound coating white chocolate-flavored buttons

MAKES 12

Break the breadsticks into thirds and put a large white marshmallow on the end of each. Melt the chocolate in a heatproof bowl set over a saucepan of simmering water. Remove the bowl from the heat and dip the marshmallows into the chocolate to cover. Use a small paintbrush to paint the chocolate down the breadsticks. Let set on wax paper.

Quick
MAKE

Sausage Mummies

MAKES 16

+ 16 chipolata sausages

+ 11-ounce (320g) package ready-rolled puff pastry

+ 1 extra large egg, beaten

+ Barbecue sauce in a squeezable bottle or tube

+ Tomato ketchup, to serve (optional)

Everyone likes sausage rolls, and puff pastry bandages transform these ones into ancient mummies. Will you choose to eat the head or body first?

VAMPIRE APPLE WEDGES

YOU WILL NEED

+ 2 red apples
+ 35 mini marshmallows
+ Smooth peanut butter

MAKES 8

Cut the apples into four pieces and remove the cores. Cut out a wedge from each piece to make a mouth. Cut the mini marshmallows in half to make fangs and attach inside the mouth with a little smooth peanut butter.

Quick **MAKE**

Dead Fly Pancakes

You will be pleased to know that the dead flies are raisins! Top with ghosts made of heavy cream and chocolate for petrifying but yummy pancakes.

MAKES 10

- ½ cup (50g) whole rolled porridge oats
- ½ cup (125ml) milk
- ¾ cup (100g) self-rising white flour
- ½ teaspoon baking powder
- ½ cup (75g) raisins
- 1 extra large egg
- Sanflower oil, for brushing
- 1¼ cups (300ml) heavy cream
- 20 chocolate chips

1. Put the oats in the milk and let soak. Meanwhile, sift the flour and baking powder into a large bowl. Stir in the raisins.

2. Make a well in the center and break in the egg. Gradually beat in the milk mixture, incorporating the flour until smooth.

3. Brush a large, nonstick frying pan or griddle with oil and heat gently. Drop tablespoons of the mixture into the pan and cook for 1–2 minutes on each side until golden. Transfer to a serving plate and let cool slightly.

4. Meanwhile, pour the cream into a bowl and, using an electric whisk, whisk until it holds its shape.

5. When the pancakes have cooled, add a dollop of the cream on top of each to look like ghosts and add two chocolate chips to look like eyes. Serve immediately.

Gruesome Green Monster Cakes

Cakes and gory frosting are colored a gruesome green—these creepy creations will be loved by all little monsters.

MAKES 12

+ 1 cup/2 sticks (240g) butter, softened
+ 1 cup (175g) superfine sugar
+ 2 extra large eggs
+ 1½ cups (175g) self-rising flour
+ 1 teaspoon baking powder
+ 5 tablespoons milk
+ Green paste food coloring
+ 2 cups (250g) confectioners' sugar
+ Red writing icing
+ 24 white chocolate buttons
+ 24 dark chocolate chips

1. Preheat the oven to 350°F/180°C/ fan 160°C/Gas Mark 4. Line a muffin pan with twelve green paper muffin cases.

2. Using an electric mixer, whisk together ½ cup/1 stick (115g) of the butter and the superfine sugar in a large bowl until light and fluffy. Beat in the eggs, one at a time. Sift in the flour and baking powder and fold into the mixture. Stir in 4 tablespoons of the milk.

3. Dip the tip of a skewer into the food coloring, add to the batter, and stir until evenly colored. Add enough to make the batter bright green. Spoon the batter evenly into the muffin cases.

4. Bake the cakes in the oven for 25 minutes until firm to the touch. Transfer to a wire rack and let cool.

5. Meanwhile, make the topping. Put the remaining butter in a large bowl and beat with a wooden spoon until smooth. Sift in the confectioners' sugar. Add the remaining 1 tablespoon milk and beat together until light and fluffy. Dip the tip of a skewer into the food coloring, add to the mixture, and stir until evenly colored.

6. When the cakes are cold, using a pastry bag fitted with a fine tip, pipe the topping on top of the cakes to make strands.

7. Pipe a little red writing icing on top of each chocolate button and use to secure a dark chocolate chip to make eyes. Place the eyes on top of the cakes.

Ghoulish Gingerbread Men

MAKES ABOUT 12

- 2¾ caps (350g) all-parpose flour
- 1 teaspoon baking soda
- 1 teaspoon ground ginger
- 1 teaspoon ground cinnamon
- ½ cap/1 stick (115g) batter
- 1 extra large egg
- 1 cap (175g) soft light brown sugar
- ⅓ cap (100g) golden syrup
- 2⅓ caps (300g) confectioners' sugar
- About 3 tablespoons water
- Chocolate writing icing, to decorate

These tombstone terrors are favorites with children and adults too! Bake a batch to decorate to look like skeletons and mummies or, if time is short, you could use bought gingerbread men.

1. Preheat the oven to 375°F/190°C/fan 170°C/Gas Mark 5. Grease several large cookie sheets. Put the flour, baking soda, ginger, cinnamon, and butter in a food processor and, using a pulsating action, blend together until the mixture forms fine bread crumbs.

2. Beat the egg in a small bowl, add to the mixture with the soft light brown sugar and syrup, and mix together to form a smooth dough.

3. Turn the dough onto a lightly floured counter and roll out thinly to a thickness of about ¼ inch (5mm). Using a gingerbread man cutter, cut out the men and place on the prepared cookie sheets. Continue until all the dough has been used.

4. Bake the cookies in the oven for 10–15 minutes, until pale golden brown. Let cool slightly for 2 minutes then transfer to a wire rack and let cool completely.

5. When cold, sift the confectioners' sugar into a large bowl, then gradually mix in the water with a wooden spoon to make a coating consistency that will coat the back of a wooden spoon.

6. Fill a piping bag, fitted with a fine writing tip, with the frosting. Pipe faces and bones to make the cookies look like skeletons and pipe lines to make them look like mummies. Use the writing icing to make their eyes.

Bubbling Witches' Cauldrons

"Double, double, toil and trouble; fire burn, and cauldron bubble." These bubbling cauldrons of green pea soup, stirred by a wicked witch, are still good enough to eat!

MAKES 12

- ½ cup/1 stick (115g) butter, softened
- 1 cup (175g) superfine sugar
- ½ teaspoon vanilla extract
- 2 extra-large eggs
- 1 cup, plus 2 tablespoons (140g) self-rising flour
- 2 tablespoons unsweetened cocoa
- 1 teaspoon baking powder
- 4 tablespoons milk
- Black paste food coloring

FOR THE TOPPING

- 3 teaspoons (15g) butter, softened
- 1¼ ounces (35g) confectioners' sugar
- ½ teaspoon milk
- Green paste or liquid food coloring
- 3½ ounces (100g) black ready-to-use rolled fondant
- Green sugared pearls
- Jellied candies, such as eyes, bones, teeth, worms, skulls, and mice
- 12 chocolate matchsticks

1. Preheat the oven to 350°F/180°C/fan 160°C/Gas Mark 4. Line a muffin pan with 12 black paper muffin cases.

2. Using an electric mixer, whisk together the butter, superfine sugar, and vanilla extract in a large bowl until light and fluffy. Beat in the eggs, one at a time. Sift in the flour, cocoa, and baking powder, and fold into the mixture. Stir in the milk.

3. Dip the tip of a skewer into the black food coloring, add to the batter, and stir until evenly colored. Add enough to make the batter as dark as possible. Spoon the batter evenly into the muffin cases.

4. Bake the cakes in the oven for 25 minutes until firm to the touch. Transfer to a wire rack and let cool.

5. Meanwhile, make the topping. Put the butter in a large bowl and beat with a wooden spoon until smooth. Sift in the confectioners' sugar. Add the milk and beat until light and fluffy. Dip the tip of a skewer into the green food coloring, add to the mixture, and stir until evenly colored.

6. When the cakes are cold, spread the topping on top of the cakes, leaving a ⅓-inch (1cm) rim around the edge.

7. Divide the fondant into 12 equal-size pieces and roll out each piece into a long sausage about 5 inches (13cm) long. Flatten each piece with the palm of your hands and place round the rim of the cakes, so that the icing is showing through the center, and seal the ends together.

8. Add sugared pearls to look like the bubbles and decorate with jellied candies. Add a chocolate matchstick to look like a stirrer.

HOOTING OWLS

Quick MAKE

YOU WILL NEED

+ 8 bought or homemade chocolate cupcakes
+ 12 ounces (350g) ready-to-use chocolate frosting
+ 8 chocolate sandwich cookies
+ 3 tablespoons ready-to-use vanilla frosting
+ 16 sugar-coated chocolates

MAKES 8

Spread the tops of bought chocolate cupcakes (or make a batch of chocolate cupcakes, omitting the black paste food coloring, as in the Bubbling Witches' Cauldrons recipe on page 22) with chocolate frosting. Very carefully twist apart the cookies. (Putting them in a microwave on high for 10 seconds helps to do this.) Spread ½ teaspoon vanilla frosting on the plain sides of each of the cookies, leaving a small border. Attach a brown or orange sugar-coated chocolate to the top of the cookies to look like the center of eyes. Attach two cookies on the upper half of the cupcakes to form eyes. Press a yellow or red sugar-coated chocolate, on its side, between the eyes to look like a beak.

FLOATING GHOSTS

Quick
MAKE

YOU WILL NEED

+ 8 round lollipops
+ 8 bought or homemade chocolate cupcakes
+ 7 ounces (250g) white ready-to-use rolled fondant
+ 16 mini chocolate chips

MAKES 8

Unwrap the lollipops and cut off a quarter of the stick. Insert the sticks into the center of bought cupcakes (or make a batch of chocolate cupcakes, omitting the black paste food coloring, as in the Bubbling Witches' Cauldrons recipe on page 22). Roll out white fondant thinly and, using a round cutter, cut out into 3¾-inch (9.5cm) circles. Put each circle over the top of the lollipops and shape it so that it looks like a draping sheet. Using a little water, attach two mini chocolate chips to each to look like eyes.

Creepy Pumpkin Faces

These spiced carrot cakes are made to look like small pumpkins with their orange frosting and licorice stems.

1 Preheat the oven to 375°F/190°C/fan 170°C/ Gas Mark 5. Line three large cookie sheets with parchment paper or grease the wells of a whoopie pan.

2 Grate the carrots and set aside. Using an electric mixer, whisk together the butter and sugar in a large bowl, until light and fluffy. Beat in the egg. Sift in the flour, baking soda, baking powder, mixed spice, and salt. Add the orange juice and reserved carrots, and stir together until combined.

3 Using a heaping tablespoon or a level 2-inch (5cm) ice-cream scoop, put the batter onto the prepared cookie sheets well apart to allow room for spreading, in 2-inch (5cm) diameter circles about 1¼ inches (3cm) high, to make 24 cakes. Alternatively, put half the batter into the prepared pan.

4 Bake in the oven for about 10 minutes, until firm to the touch. Transfer to a wire rack and let cool. Repeat if you are using a whoopie pan.

5 Meanwhile, make the topping. Put the butter and cream cheese in a large bowl and beat together with a wooden spoon until light and fluffy. Sift in the confectioners' sugar and beat together until combined. Dip the tip of a skewer into the food coloring, add to the mixture, and stir until evenly colored.

6 When the cakes are cold, spread the mixture on top of the cakes. Using the blade of a knife, run lines down the tops to look like pumpkin skin.

7 Use the writing icing to make eyes, a nose, and mouth on each cake. Cut the licorice twists in half and stick a piece in the top of each cake to make a stem. Place on top of the bottom halves to make pumpkins.

Scary Rats

MAKES 8

+ 8 ounces (225g) black ready-to-use rolled fondant
+ Red writing icing
+ Seedless raspberry jam
+ 8 round semisweet chocolate chip cookies

Ramp up the fear factor with these revolting rats. Made from black-colored fondant and nestling in a pool of jam, at least these creepy critters won't be spreading any germs! Use brown ready-to-use rolled fondant to make brown rats. Either color will taste delicious but don't forget to bite the heads off first, if you dare, to kill them!

1. Roll the fondant into 8 equal-size balls, reserving about ½ ounce (15g).

2. Pinch one end of each ball into a point to look like a nose. Pull and pinch the other end into a long, thin tail.

3. Roll the reserved fondant into small balls and press flat. Use a little water to attach them to the rats' heads to look like ears.

4. Using red writing icing, add dots to look like eyes. Let the rats dry overnight.

5. Spread a little seedless raspberry jam onto the center of the cookies and attach the rats so that they look as though they are sitting in a pool of blood.

SPOOKY RUBY RED ORANGES

Quick MAKE

YOU WILL NEED

+ 5-ounce (140g) package raspberry gelatin dessert
+ 8 oranges or munchkin pumpkins

MAKES 8

Make up a package of raspberry gelatin following the package directions. Slice the top off the oranges or munchkin pumpkins and carefully scoop out the inside flesh. Very carefully take a thin slice off the bottom, without cutting into the orange or pumpkin, so that they will stand up. Put the oranges or pumkins on a plate. Pour the gelatin into the oranges or pumpkins and let set in the refrigerator. When set, using a sharp knife, carefully carve the eyes into the orange or pumpkin skin.

GHASTLY GRAPE EYEBALLS

YOU WILL NEED

* 10 green grapes
* 10 white mini marshmallows
* Chocolate writing icing

MAKES 20

Cut the grapes in half and top each rounded surface with a mini marshmallow, cut in half. Using the writing icing, pipe pupils in the center of each.

Quick **MAKE**

Chomping Monster Cookies

These refrigerator golden raisin cookies are looking at you and are ready to chomp!

MAKES 10

- 1¾ caps (225g) all-purpose floar, plas extra for dusting
- 1 teaspoon baking powder
- ½ cap/1 stick (115g) batter, plas extra for greasing
- 1 cap (175g) superfine sagar
- ⅓ cap (55g) golden raisins
- 1 extra large egg, beaten
- 14 oances (400g) ready-to-ase vanilla frosting
- 3 paste or liqaid food colorings, such as red, green, orange, or parple
- ¼ cap (50g) white chocolate chips
- 20 mini sagar-coated chocolates

32

1 Put the flour and baking powder in a food processor. Add the butter, cut into small pieces and, using a pulsating action, blend until the mixture forms fine bread crumbs. Add the sugar and golden raisins and stir together. Add the egg and stir together to form a dough.

2 Turn the dough out onto a lightly floured counter and shape into a log about 2 inches (5cm) in diameter. Wrap the log in wax paper and then foil and chill in the refrigerator for at least 8 hours or overnight.

3 Preheat the oven to 375°F/190°C/fan 170°C/Gas Mark 5. Grease two large cookie sheets.

4 Slice the dough into ½-inch (1cm) circles, to make 20 cookies, and put on the cookie sheets, keeping them well apart to allow room for spreading. If preferred, you can make fewer cookies and store the log in the refrigerator for up to one week or in the freezer for longer. If storing in the freezer, slice and bake from frozen.

5 Bake in the oven for about 10 minutes until lightly golden. Let cool for 5 minutes and then transfer to a wire rack and let cool completely.

6 Meanwhile, divide the frosting between three bowls. Dip the tip of a skewer into one of the food colorings, add to one of the mixtures, and stir until evenly colored. Add enough to make the mixture a bright color. Repeat with the other two mixtures.

7 When the cookies are cold, use the frostings to sandwich two cookies together, reserving a little frosting to attach the decorations. Put the top cookies at an angle so that they touch on one side and are open on the other side to look like an open mouth.

8 Arrange the white chocolate chips in the frosting to look like teeth. Using the reserved frosting, attach sugar-coated chocolates to look like eyes.

Scurrying Chocolate Mice

You might not like real mice but you will love these chocolate ones! These little squeakers are delicious chocolate-covered cakes.

MAKES 12

- 10½ ounces (300g) bought Madeira cake
- 5 teaspoons (25g) butter, softened
- ¼ cup (55g) whole cream cheese
- ½ cup (60g) confectioners' sugar
- 9 ounces (250g) compound coating semisweet chocolate-flavored buttons
- 24 blanched almonds
- White writing icing
- 12 licorice laces

34

1 Line a cookie sheet with wax paper. Break the cake into a large bowl and crumble with your fingers to form fine crumbs. Add the butter and cream cheese and mix well together. Sift in the sugar and mix together until combined.

2 Shape the mixture into 12 even-size oval shapes and press together firmly. Place on the prepared cookie sheet and chill in the refrigerator for 30 minutes until firm.

3 Put the chocolate into a heatproof bowl. Stand the bowl over a saucepan of simmering water, making sure that the bottom of the bowl doesn't touch the water, and heat, stirring occasionally, until the chocolate has melted. Remove the bowl from the heat.

4 Using a skewer at one end to hold each cake, dip each one into the chocolate until it is coated. Let any excess drip back into the bowl and then return the cake to the cookie sheet. Quickly press two almonds into the head of each mouse to look like ears. Repeat with the remaining cakes.

5 Use the white writing icing to pipe eyes and insert a licorice lace where the skewer was to look like a tail. Leave in a cool place for 1 hour until set.

Crawling Spiders

Creepy, crawly spiders are often feared as they run into hiding, but there's nothing to be scared of when you take a bite of these large chocolate whoopie cake spiders.

MAKES 24

- 1¼ cups/2½ sticks (290g) butter, softened, plus extra for greasing
- 1 cup packed (200g) dark soft brown sugar
- 1¼ teaspoons vanilla extract
- 1 extra large egg
- 2¼ cups (280g) all-purpose flour
- ½ cup (50g) unsweetened cocoa
- 1¼ teaspoons baking soda
- Pinch of salt
- 1 cup (225ml) buttermilk
- 2¾ cups (350g) confectioners' sugar
- 1 tablespoon milk
- Red paste or liquid food coloring
- Two 2¼-ounce (75g) packages strawberry or licorice laces
- 48 jelly beans

1. To make the spiders, preheat the oven to 375°F/190°C/fan 170°C/Gas Mark 5. Line three large cookie sheets with parchment paper or grease the wells of a whoopie pan.

2. Using an electric mixer, whisk together ½ cup/1 stick (115g) butter, the brown sugar, and 1 teaspoon vanilla extract in a large bowl, until light and fluffy. Beat in the egg. Sift in the flour, cocoa, baking soda, and salt. Add the buttermilk and stir together until combined.

3. Using a heaping tablespoon or a level 2-inch (5cm) ice-cream scoop, put the batter onto the prepared cookie sheets, well apart to allow room for spreading, in 2-inch (5cm) diameter circles about 1¼ inches (3cm) high, to make 24 cakes. Alternatively, put half the batter into the prepared pan.

4. Bake in the oven for about 10 minutes, until firm to the touch. Transfer to a wire rack and let cool. Repeat if you are using a whoopie pan.

5. Meanwhile, make the topping. Put the remaining ¾ cup/1½ sticks (175g) butter and the remaining ¼ teaspoon vanilla extract in a large bowl and beat together with a wooden spoon until smooth. Sift in the confectioners' sugar. Add the milk and beat together until light and fluffy. Dip the tip of a skewer into the food coloring, add to the mixture, and stir until evenly colored.

6. When the cakes are cold, cut the laces into 96 lengths to make legs. Lay four across each cake and spread the topping on top to secure the legs. Add two jelly beans to each to look like eyes.

Beastly Bat Cookies

Which is your favorite—chocolate chip or chocolate cookies? You don't need to decide with these two-in-one cookies. These may look like bats, but fortunately they are unable to fly... According to a Halloween myth, if a bat flew into your house on Halloween it meant it was haunted, because ghosts had let it in!

MAKES 16

FOR THE CHOCOLATE COOKIES
- 5 tablespoons (70g) butter, softened
- ½ cup (100g) superfine sugar
- 1 extra large egg
- ½ teaspoon vanilla extract
- ⅔ cup (75g) all-purpose flour
- ¼ cup (20g) unsweetened cocoa
- ¼ teaspoon baking soda
- Pinch of salt

FOR THE CHOCOLATE CHIP COOKIES
- ½ cup/1 stick (115g) butter, softened
- ½ cup (85g) superfine sugar
- ½ cup (85g) packed light soft brown sugar
- 1 extra large egg
- 1 teaspoon vanilla extract
- 1¼ cups (150g) all-purpose flour
- ½ teaspoon baking soda
- Pinch of salt
- 6 ounces (175g) semisweet chocolate chunks

TO DECORATE
- Pink marshmallows
- Chocolate frosting

1 First make the chocolate cookies. Using an electric mixer, whisk together the butter and sugar in a large bowl until light and fluffy. Beat in the egg and vanilla extract. Sift in the flour, cocoa, baking soda, and salt and fold into the batter.

2 Preheat the oven to 350°F/180°C/fan 160°C/Gas Mark 4. Line two large cookie sheets with parchment paper. Take a heaping tablespoon of the batter and, using your hands, form each piece of dough into a ball. Place on the prepared cookie sheets, keeping them well apart to allow room for spreading. Continue to make 16 cookies.

3 Bake in the oven for 10–15 minutes until set. Let cool for 5 minutes and then transfer to a wire rack and let cool completely.

4 To make the chocolate chip cookies, using an electric mixer, whisk together the butter, superfine, and brown sugar in a large bowl until light and fluffy. Beat in the egg and vanilla extract. Sift in the flour, baking soda, and salt and fold into the batter. Stir in the chocolate chunks.

5 Increase the oven temperature to 375°F/ 190°C/fan 170°C/Gas Mark 5. Line two large cookie sheets with parchment paper. Drop heaping tablespoons onto the prepared cookie sheets, keeping them well apart to allow

room for spreading, to make 16 cookies. Flatten them slightly with the back of a spoon.

6 Bake in the oven for 10–15 minutes, until lightly golden.

7 As soon as the chocolate chip cookies are cooked, insert marshmallows to look like eyes. Transfer to a wire rack and let cool completely.

8 When cold, break the chocolate cookies in half. Using a little chocolate frosting, attach two chocolate cookie halves, at an angle, to each chocolate chip cookie to look like bats' wings.

BLOODSTAINED BRAINS

YOU WILL NEED

+ *Red and black icing paste or liquid food coloring*
+ *12 ounces (350g) ready-to-use vanilla frosting*
+ *8 chocolate cupcakes or red velvet cupcakes*

MAKES 8

Dip the tip of a skewer into red paste or liquid food coloring and add to the frosting. Repeat with black paste or liquid food coloring and stir until the mixture is brain-colored pinkish gray. Be careful not to add too much. Pipe the frosting on top of eight bought chocolate cupcakes or make a batch of red velvet cupcakes, as in the Wizards' Trick-or-Treat Cupcakes recipe on page 8. Dip the tip of a skewer into the red food coloring and draw red veins on the frosting to look like blood.

Quick
MAKE

SNARLING STRAWBERRY SNAKE

Quick MAKE

YOU WILL NEED

+ *8 strawberries*
+ *2 bananas*
+ *Strawberry lace*
+ *Chocolate writing icing*
+ *Lemon juice, for brushing (optional)*

MAKES 1

Thickly slice the strawberries and bananas. Arrange them on a plate to make a snake shape. To make the snake's head, cut out a wedge from a strawberry to make a mouth, insert a length of strawberry lace or small piece of strawberry to make a tongue, and pipe on chocolate writing icing to make eyes. Serve at once or brush with lemon juice to stop the bananas turning brown.

Peanut Butter Pumpkins

Balls of peanut butter cookies are sprinkled with orange sugar crystals to look just like squashed mini pumpkins, but are much tastier to eat!

MAKES ABOUT 24

- ½ cap/1 stick (115g) batter, softened
- ½ cap (115g) smooth peanut batter
- ½ cap (115g) superfine sagar
- ½ cap (115g) packed soft light brown sagar
- 1 egg
- 1¼ caps (150g) all-parpose floar
- 1¾ oances (50g) orange sagar crystals
- 6 pretzels
- 2 tablespoons water
- 2 teaspoons green liquid food coloring
- ¾ cap (50g) dry answeetened coconat

1 Preheat the oven to 375°F/190°C/fan 170°C/ Gas Mark 5. Line two large cookie sheets with parchment paper.

2 Using an electric mixer, whisk together the butter, peanut butter, superfine, and brown sugar in a large bowl until light and fluffy. Beat in the egg. Sift in the flour and fold into the batter.

3 Sprinkle the orange crystals onto a plate. Take a heaping tablespoon of the batter and, using your hands, form each piece of dough into a ball. Roll in the crystals and then put on the prepared cookie sheet. Continue to make about 24 balls. Using a blunt knife, make lines down the sides of the cookies to look like pumpkin ridges. Break the pretzels into small pieces and press into the top of each ball to make a stem.

4 Bake in the oven for 10–15 minutes until the pumpkins are lightly golden. Let cool for 5 minutes and then transfer to a wire rack and let cool completely.

5 Meanwhile, put the water and food coloring in a large resealable plastic bag. Add the coconut and shake together until evenly colored, adding more water and more food coloring if necessary. If the coconut is very wet, spread it out on paper towels and let dry.

6 Sprinkle the green coconut on a plate to look like grass and put the pumpkins on top to serve.

Black Cat Brownies

Found in the company of witches, people used to say that a black cat brings bad luck and mischief, but now it is considered good luck for one to cross your path. These brownies will bring nothing but joy to anyone who eats one!

MAKES 12

+ ¾ cup/1½ sticks (175g) butter, plus extra for greasing

+ 6 ounces (175g) semisweet chocolate (minimum 70% cocoa solids)

+ Generous 1 packed cup (250g) soft light brown sugar

+ 3 extra large eggs

+ 1 teaspoon vanilla extract

+ Scant 1 cup (115g) all-purpose flour

+ Generous ¼ cup (50g) milk chocolate buttons

+ Generous ¼ cup (50g) white chocolate buttons

+ 2 tablespoons water

+ 2 tsp green liquid food coloring

+ Scant 1 cup (75g) dry unsweetened coconut

+ 12 black cat capcake picks

44

1. Preheat the oven to 350°F/180°C/fan 160°C. Butter a square 8-inch (20cm) brownie pan and line with baking parchment.

2. Break the chocolate into a heatproof bowl and add the butter, cut into small pieces. Set the bowl over a saucepan of simmering water and heat, stirring occasionally, until the butter has melted. Stir together until smooth then add the sugar. Remove the bowl from the heat and let cool slightly.

3. Beat together the eggs and vanilla extract. When the chocolate mixture has cooled, add the eggs and beat together. Add the flour and fold into the chocolate mixture. Add the chocolate buttons and stir together until combined. Turn the batter into the prepared pan.

4. Bake in the oven for about 40 minutes, or until the top is firm but the center is still slightly wobbly. Do not overcook as the cake will continue to cook as it cools. Let cool in the pan.

5. Put 1 teaspoon water and the food coloring in a large resealable plastic bag. Add the coconut and shake together until evenly colored, adding more water and more food coloring if necessary. If the coconut is very wet, spread it out on paper towels and let dry.

6. Cut the cake into 12 squares and sprinkle the coconut on top to look like grass. Add a black cat pick to each brownie.

MAGIC WIZARDS' WANDS

YOU WILL NEED

+ 6 ounces (175g) compound coating white chocolate-flavored buttons
+ 12 breadsticks
+ Sparkling cake decorations

MAKES 12

Melt the chocolate-flavored buttons in a heatproof bowl set over a saucepan of simmering water, making sure that the bottom of the bowl doesn't touch the water, or in a microwave. Remove the bowl from the heat and dip one end of the breadsticks, one at a time, into the chocolate to cover. Put on wax paper and sprinkle all over with a variety of sparkling cake decorations, such as sprinkles, sugar crystals, and silver candied balls. Let set.

Quick MAKE